The GOLDEN AGE *of* AVIATION

KATHERINE S. WILLIAMSON

SMITHMARK

For my grandfather, J. P. Williamson,
and my father, J. P. Williamson, Jr.

ACKNOWLEDGMENTS

Many thanks to J. P. Williamson, Jr., Doris Palmer, John Downing, Antonia Felix, Cynthia Sternau, Anne and Tom Glisson, Ray Brooks, Gerry Braun, Ulrich Brinkmann, Denise Bergstrom, Tom McCarthy, Marie Drumm, Pat Barnett, Claudia Chadbourne, Fern Gorin, the Staff at the Science and Technology Center of the New York Public Library, and the community of St. Peter's Episopal Church in Chelsea.

This edition published in 1996 by SMITHMARK Publishers, a division of U.S. Media Holdings, Inc.
16 East 32nd Street
New York, NY 10016

SMITHMARK books are available for bulk purchase for sales promotion and premium use.

For details write or call the manager of special sales, SMITHMARK Publishers
16 East 32nd Street
New York, NY 10016
(212) 532-6600

This book was designed and produced by Todtri Productions Limited
P.O. Box 572
New York, NY 10116-0572
FAX: (212) 279-1241

Printed and bound in Singapore

Library of Congress Catalog Card Number 96-68014
ISBN 0-7651-9775-8

Author: Katherine S. Williamson

Publisher: Robert M. Tod
Editorial Director: Elizabeth Loonan
Designer and Art Director: Ron Pickless
Production Coordinator: Heather Weigel
Senior Editor: Edward Douglas
Project Editor: Cynthia Sternau
Associate Editor: Shawna Kimber
Picture Researchers: Julie Dewitt, Natalie Goldstein,
    Kate Lewin, Cathy Stastny
Research Assistant: Laura Wyss
Typeset and DTP: Blanc Verso/UK

PICTURE CREDITS

Art Resource/Alinari p. 9

Art Resource/Giraudon pp. 10-11, 13, 18

J. Allan Cash Ltd p. 31

Corbis-Bettmann pp. 7, 14 (bottom), 21 (top), 37, 47 (bottom), 48(top), 48 (bottom), 50, 52, 53, 56 (bottom), 60 (top), 65 (top)

Mary Evans Picture Library pp. 4, 6, 8, 12, 17, 19, 22 (bottom), 23, 26, 36, 38 (bottom), 39, 40, 41 (top), 44, 45, 46, 49, 51, 58, 59, 62, 66 (top), 67, 72, 73

William B. Folsom p. 76 (top)

Hulton Deutsch Collection Ltd pp. 15, 32 (top), 33 (bottom), 34 (top), 34 (bottom)

Mirror Syndication International pp. 5, 42, 57, 60 (bottom), 61, 64 (top), 64 (bottom), 66 (bottom)

New York Public Library pp. 16, 25, 65 (bottom)

Chris Taylor/Sylvia Cordaiy Photo Library Ltd p. 24

Topham Picture Source pp. 20 (top), 20 (bottom), 21 (bottom), 22 (top), 27, 28, 29, 30, 32 (bottom), 33 (top), 38 (top), 41 (bottom), 42 (top), 43, 47 (top), 54, 55, 56 (top), 63, 70 (top), 70 (bottom), 74 (top), 74 (bottom), 75, 77, 78

UPI/Corbis-Bettman p. 69, 71

Wright Brothers National Memorial Museum p. 14 (top)

CONTENTS

*I*NTRODUCTION

*F*rom 1903 up until the eve of World War II, flying was glamorous and new, and it struck a chord in the hearts of some of the most intelligent and adventurous people in the world. More than a form of transportation, flying was a vehicle for individual effort and expression, and early aviators put their souls into developing machines that would fly. They did the job so well, in fact, that airplanes have become a way of life we take for granted today.

The early days of aviation were a time when flying was more than a business, it was a passion. When flying was still new, many people who had the chance to fly rhapsodized over the mystery and the beauty of the experience, for they saw the new technology as having a soul.

Airplanes have lost much of their magic in the past fifty years. Today's commercial jumbo jets may appear to be nothing more than efficient machines, but they, too, were born in the hearts and minds of people.

Opposite: Italian aviators Arturo Ferrarin and Carlo del Prete made the first non-stop flight from Rome to Brazil in 1928. The 4,340-mile (7,000-kilometer) journey took forty-four hours.

Below: The interior of the German Dornier Do-X flying boat was more spacious than the *Graf Zeppelin*. Both aircraft were the largest in the world in 1929.

Left: American aviator Amelia Earhart smiles as she stands in front of her plane. The cause of Earhart's disappearance over the Pacific Ocean in 1937 is still a mystery.

Indeed, they have a proud and colorful lineage dating back to a time when piston engines, not jets, powered airplanes, and flying literally captivated the world.

The dream of flying has fueled the human imagination since ancient times. Many cultures have legends of brave mortals who soared through the sky like birds, and the most famous of these is the myth of Daedalus and Icarus. Daedalus was a great builder who lost favor with Minos, the king of Crete, and was imprisoned in an isolated island tower, along with his son Icarus. The king kept strict watch over the land and sea, so Daedalus fashioned huge wings with which to escape by air. Sewing large feathers onto a frame, he adhered smaller feathers to it with beeswax, and the finished wings had the gentle curvature of a bird's.

Daedalus strapped his creation on his son's back, and taught him how to flap the wings like a bird, warning him to keep to a moderate height, for if he flew too low the spray from the sea would clog his wings, and if he flew too high, the heat of the sun would melt them. Icarus jumped from the tower and, exhilarated by the sensation, he flew higher and higher, but as his father had predicted, the wax finally melted and he plunged to his death in the sea.

The myth of Icarus was intended to remind all who heard the tale that they were humans, not gods, but it also has something more to say about the pioneers of aviation. Like Icarus, the first aviators were in constant danger of flying too high or low for their own safety, yet if they had not dared to fly at all, humanity would have missed out on one of the greatest adventures of all time.

Opposite: Well-wishers bearing France's Tricolor and the British Red Ensign welcome France's Louis Bleriot to the cliffs of Dover. On July 25, 1909, Bleriot became the first person to fly a plane across the English Channel.

L'Assiette au Beurre

REDACTION ET ADMINISTRATION PARIS

L'ANNÉE 1908

revue d'en haut

Vole Wright!...

Chapter One

*L*EARNING TO FLY

It took thousands of years for people to realize that wings that flap actually work best for birds and insects—not for human flying machines. In 1804, a brilliant amateur scientist in Britain named Sir George Cayley finally designed a glider with wings that did not flap, or "fixed" wings. Cayley's glider worked, and for the first time human flight became possible in a craft heavier than air.

Inventors continued to experiment with Cayley's fixed-wing gliders throughout the nineteenth century. In the 1890s, Otto Lilienthal, a German civil engineer, constructed sturdy gliders made of willow and bamboo covered with taut cotton fabric. No one at that time had made as many successful glider flights as Lilienthal, who completed nearly two thousand flights from the Rhinowar Hills, as well as from a cone-shaped hill he built

Opposite: This magazine cover from 1908 depicts the admiration between American aviator Wilbur Wright and the French people as a love affair between a man and a woman. In reality, the Wright brothers were extremely proper, and never married.

Below: In this depiction of the Greek myth, Daedalus watches his son Icarus fall to his death.

near Berlin. Lilienthal died in 1896 when he fell 50 feet (15 meters) from one of his gliders.

Octave Chanute, an American engineer and aviator, helped turn Lilienthal into a hero at the turn of the century. Chanute also encouraged young aviators. By the late 1890s he was corresponding with two brothers named Wilbur and Orville Wright, who were building gliders in their bicycle shop in Dayton, Ohio.

Chanute did have dreams of his own, though. Like many aviators at the turn of the century, he wanted to be responsible for the first sustained powered flight in a craft of his own design. Chanute experimented with several Lilienthal-type gliders, and he built his most successful one in 1896, the same year that Lilienthal died. It featured external trusses in the form of wires that held the two wings to the main body of the aircraft. Chanute had used the same type of support when he built the Kansas City Bridge, the first bridge across the Missouri River.

Chanute's fixed wing biplane glider never flew under its own power as he had hoped it would, but it became the model for the Wright brothers' powered glider, the Flyer. As such, it was the prototype for the most popular airplane body in the early days of aviation.

A WHOPPER FLYING MACHINE

The weather was cold and windy on the isolated coast of North Carolina, known as the Outer Banks, the day Orville and Wilbur Wright flew their

Above: The Wright brothers' *Flyer* leaves the beach at Kitty Hawk, North Carolina the morning of December 17, 1903. Wilbur watches as his younger brother Orville pilots the first sustained, mechanically powered flight in history.

Right: During a test flight in 1908 Orville Wright's co-pilot Lieutenant Thomas Selfridge became the first person to die in a powered aircraft crash.

Above: In 1909, a Wright brothers'
plane looks like a shepherd from
a distant future in flight over a
flock of sheep in Italy.

mechanically-powered glider for the first time. It was the week before
Christmas, December 17, 1903. Conditions were not ideal for flying the
delicate craft made of cotton and wood, but the Wright brothers wanted
one last try before they headed home to Ohio. They would not return to
the fishing village of Kitty Hawk, where they had tested their gliders for
three years, until the next spring. The brothers carried their plane down to
the beach that morning, and Orville, the younger of the two, had the honor
of flying what they called their "whopper flying machine" first. They
poured gasoline into the four-cylinder, water-cooled engine they had
designed themselves and built in Dayton. They placed the battery on the
wing, and hooked its wires to the engine. Two 8-foot (2.5-meter) propellers
were attached to the engine with bicycle chains, and mounted behind the
Flyer's wings to push it forward.

Orville lay down in the hip cradle next to the engine on the lower wing.
In a strong headwind, the Flyer skidded off the 60-foot (18-meter) wooden
rail the brothers had laid on the beach, lifted less than a few feet into the
air, and remained airborne for twelve seconds. It was a short flight, but in
those twelve seconds the Wright brothers fulfilled man's ancient longing to
fly. They were the first to solve all the problems of mechanically-powered
flight, and they did it largely on their own. But the hardest part was yet to
come—they had to convince people to buy their invention.

The Wright brothers offered to build the Flyer, the first airplane and the
best in the world at the time, for the United States government in 1905, but

FIRST IN AMERICA
AVIATION MEET
LOS
ANGELE
JANUAR
10-20
1910
American & Foreign
Aviators
DAILY FLIGHTS

Right: In 1910, Los Angeles billed its international aviation meet as the first in the United States. The Aero Club of New York hosted the same type of event in 1909 with less fanfare.

Opposite: Airplanes at the week-long air show in Betheny, France in 1909 competed for a greater prize than speed or altitude. Airplane manufacturers used the shows to promote their designs as the standard airplane body.

there was no interest in their proposal. Few people outside the fledgling field of aviation had the foresight in 1905 to recognize the enormous potential of the airplane. Orville Wright demonstrated a newer version of the Flyer to members of Congress in the summer of 1908, but Wilbur was not with him. He was in France demonstrating the Flyer to the public for the first time ever.

On August 8, 1908, Wilbur flew the Flyer in front of about sixty

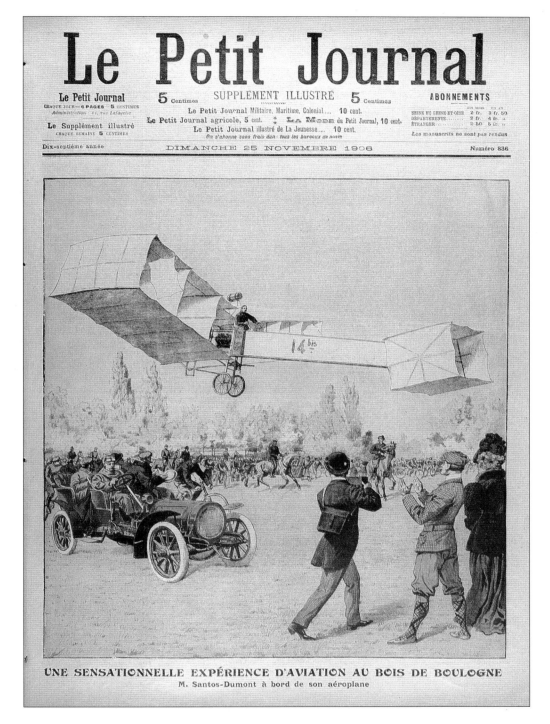

Le Petit Journal

SUPPLEMENT ILLUSTRÉ

UNE SENSATIONNELLE EXPÉRIENCE D'AVIATION AU BOIS DE BOULOGNE
M. Santos-Dumont à bord de son aéroplane

Left: Alberto Santos-Dumont flew his box-kite plane *14-bis* over Paris' Bois de Boulogne in 1906. A hero in his native Brazil as well as in France, Santos-Dumont was the first person to sustain powered flight in Europe that same year.

spectators at a racetrack near LeMans, France. The crowd of aristocrats, aviators, and wealthy vacationers jumped to their feet in unison when the Flyer took off. It turned beautifully, it climbed and descended reliably, and it even landed at their feet.

French aviators, several of whom were in the crowd that day, had already made many landmark flights, and were on the verge of achieving more. Alberto Santos-Dumont, a Brazilian who lived in France, made the first heavier-than-air flight in Europe in his box-kite plane, *14 bis*, in 1906. Two months after Wilbur Wright's first flight in France, Henri Farman would fly his Voisin glider from the town of Chalons to Reims, 16 miles (25 kilometers) away, a feat so daring that even the Wrights had not attempted it. But the sophisticated crowd that had gathered that August day near Le

Opposite: The French brought elegance to aviation as illustrated by this poster for the 1910 air meet in Nice on the French Riviera. In a streamlined Bleriot monoplane, the pilot throws roses to the wind above one of the most picturesque towns in France.

Opposite top: Harriet Quimby, the first American woman to receive a pilot's license, climbs into her Moisant monoplane in 1912. That same year she became the first woman to fly solo across the English channel.

Opposite below: A pilot with a mailbag beneath his Valkyrie tail-first monoplane prepares to take off from Hendon Field near London in 1911. The flight was a rehearsal for Great Britain's first air mail service that began a few days later.

Right: Shown here is the start of the first air race at Hendon Field near London. Hendon hosted races for the public regularly until the eve of the Second World War, when the R.A.F. began to practice military maneuvers there in private.

Below right: Roland Garros of France prepares to fly from London to Paris in his Morane-Saulnier monoplane years before the first airline flew the route in 1919. He was the first pilot to fly across the Mediterranean Sea in 1913.

Overleaf top: The inventor of the flying boat, American airplane designer Glenn Curtiss, displays his 1913 flying boat in Brighton, England. Placing the 80-horsepower Curtiss engine under the top wing was an improvement that reduced propellor spray during takeoff.

Mans had never seen an airplane fly with the control of the Wright brothers' plane. Wilbur Wright became an overnight success, and Europe went mad for aviation, as it had over a hundred years before when the Montgolfier brothers invented the hot air balloon. Wilbur's demonstration flights that summer galvanized the French aviation community; one year later the French had improved their aircraft so dramatically that their planes and pilots were among the best in the world.

THE REIMS AIR MEET

In August of 1909, Reims hosted the world's first international air meet. For one week, thirty-five single-engined airplanes chugged in the sky. Two hundred thousand people paid to witness the (mostly French) pilots set records for altitude, speed, and passenger carrying, only to be surpassed the next day. An estimated one hundred thousand more watched from the surrounding hills.

   Reims drew entrants from Great Britain and the United States, but the French took most of the records in French planes. Henri Farman made the first flight of over 100 miles (160 kilometers) in his biplane, breaking Wilbur Wright's recent record. Farman's plane also featured something

Above: France's Hubert Latham crashed into the English Channel when he attempted to cross it in 1909. When rescuers found him smoking a cigarette on the downed plane, his coolness under pressure charmed his countrymen.

Opposite below: A cow attacks an early French aviator who lands in her field. Pastures served as airfields for many pilots around the world in 1910, when this drawing was made.

new: moveable sections of the wings, called ailerons, for controlling flight.

French pilot Hubert Latham spiraled to a height of 503 feet (153 meters) in his graceful Antoinette monoplane and won the prize for altitude. He also set a speed record of 42 miles per hour (67 kilometers per hour) over the 100-kilometer (62-mile) course.

Latham's plane was one of the streamlined flying machines the French were pioneering at the time. The wing supports were enclosed in a body that tapered to a point in the rear; this type of construction provided lower resistance to air, and increased the plane's speed.

The lone American entrant in the Reims Air Show, Glenn Curtiss, was known in the United States as the world's fastest man, from a record for motorcycle speed he set in Ormand Beach, Florida, in 1906. In a pusher biplane of his own design, the *Reims Racer*, Curtiss won the race that capped the week at Reims: the 20-kilometer (12-mile) Gordon Bennet cup race. He flew 47 miles per hour (75 kilometers per hour), beating French aviator Louis Bleriot in his Bleriot monoplane by six seconds, and earning the distinction of the fastest man in the air. But the world had not heard the last of Bleriot—one year later he became the first person to pilot the English Channel in a craft heavier than air.

WINGWALKING AND
LOOPING THE LOOP

After Reims, air shows, races, and meets sprang up around the world, and introduced thousands of people to the airplane. They were usually held at racetracks (many of which evolved into airfields) or grass fields, since airfields were not common until well into the 1930s.

The men and women who flew in the early air shows were great acrobatic pilots who performed death-defying stunts to the delight of spectators. And no air show was complete without at least one pilot swooping low over the

Left: The Lebaudy brothers' 1903 airship was nicknamed *Le Jaune* for its yellow cloth coating. Its 38-mile (61-kilometer) flight from Moisson to Paris on November 12, 1903 was the first controlled journey by a practical dirigible.

Above: A French Spad downs a German plane in 1918 during an aerial battle in World War I.

crowds, making ladies swoon, and men grab their hats.

Stunt pilot Adolphe Pegoud was a favorite at air shows in Paris and London. On September 2, 1913, Pegoud flew a plane upside down for the first time in history. A couple of weeks later he succeeded in "looping the loop"—flying his special Bleriot monoplane around in a vertical circle.

Many early stunt pilots found work on the exhibition teams that manufacturers formed to promote their planes. The two largest manufacturers in the United States before the First World War, the Wright and Curtiss companies, sponsored teams of pilots who performed daredevil stunts like wingwalking, climbing down a ladder into a moving car, and changing planes in mid-air. The work was so dangerous that of the original five flyers on the Wright team, only one survived the two-year contract.

Clubs devoted to aviation, called aero clubs, were established in the major flying countries before the war, with the most venerable of them all in France. These clubs staged some of the most exciting air meets of the early days of aviation.

In 1911, the prestigious Aero Club of America, headquartered in an elegant Manhattan townhouse, sponsored a meet at the Belmont racetrack that had all the elements the public craved: fast aircraft, new aircraft from across the Atlantic, and something extra—female pilots. Harriet Quimby, who had recently received the first pilot's license granted to a woman in the United States, flew in the meet, as did her friend, Matilde Moisant, the second American woman to receive her pilot's license.

Quimby had a brief but illustrious flying career with the Moisant family's

exhibition team in the United States and Mexico. In 1912, a few months after she had piloted her Bleriot monoplane across the English Channel—the first woman to do so—Quimby fell from her plane to her death in Boston Harbor during the Boston Harvard Air Meet. If her open-cockpit plane had had seat belts, she and her passenger might have survived the turbulent ride.

Above: In 1918, Dutch airplane designer Tony Fokker produced Germany's most successful fighter plane of the First World War. The red, black, and white Fokker D.VII reached speeds greater than 125 m.p.h. (201 k.p.h.) at 15,000 feet (4,570 meters).

SEAPLANES AND AIRSHIPS

Two other aircraft developed alongside the land-based airplane: dirigibles, or airships, and airplanes based on water. The cigar-shaped dirigible was a lighter-than-air craft which evolved from the technology of hot air balloons. (The term "dirigible" refers to the airship's ability to be directed or steered.) A boat builder from the French port of Marseilles, Henri Fabre, invented the first seaplane, or floatplane in 1910 (a seaplane is an aircraft with floats or pontoons, whereas a flying boat is an airplane whose fuselage or main body actually floats in the water like the hull of a boat), and American airplane designer Glenn Curtiss pioneered the flying boat in 1911.

Flying boats and seaplanes soon became the fastest planes in the air. In 1913, French aviator and race-car driver Jacques Schneider organized a race in Monaco for water-based aircraft. It was a French Deperdussin monoplane fitted with floats that won the trophy that year, but by the 1920s, the Schneider Trophy had become the most prestigious of all the international air races.

In the early 1900s the British and the Germans began experimenting with airships. Britain's airship program seemed doomed from the beginning, for the first rigid airship, with a metal covering surrounding the inner balloon, crumpled when it was being removed from its floating shed in 1911. The ship, named the *Mayfly*, and built by Vickers for the Navy, proved to be damaged beyond repair, and it never flew.

The German experience with airships was quite different. Count Ferdinand von Zeppelin invented the rigid airship in 1906, and for the next thirty years his company built the best and biggest airships in the world. In 1910 the Zeppelin airship became the first passenger-carrying aircraft in the world. The *Schwaben* was DELAG airline's first successful Zeppelin. Its passenger gondola looked like a first-class railroad coach, with mahogany paneling and mother-of-pearl inlays. Between 1911 and 1914, DELAG's Zeppelin fleet carried 34,028 passengers over 100,000 miles (160,900 kilometers) between towns in Germany.

Count von Zeppelin actually had a far less peaceful use in mind for his invention, which could travel long distances and stay aloft for up to

Below: Helpers push a French Spad in the snow during the First World War. The Spad was strong and fast, and the S.VII reached speeds of 118 m.p.h. (190 k.p.h.) in 1916.

twenty-four hours, for the Zeppelin was to play a key role in the air combat of World War I.

THE FIRST AIR WAR

In August of 1914, when the First World War began, there were not enough planes or pilots in all of Europe to make up an aviation branch of the military. The flimsy, unarmed machines that had performed in air shows in Europe became the nucleus of Europe's flying force. The Allied armies saw the airplane as a novelty, useful mainly for reconnaissance duty.

But a little bat-winged German plane called a Taube (Dove) quickly changed that idea, when Taubes dropped the first bombs of the war on Britain in 1914.

Zeppelin attacks by night followed the Taubes in 1915. These giant, silent airships terrorized the British, and their incendiary bombs killed hundreds of people. But Britain developed fighter planes and incendiary bullets, and chased the Zeppelins off by 1917.

At the start of the war Count von Zeppelin turned his genius to making bomber planes, and in 1915 the twin-engined Gotha appeared. The Gotha

Above: A group of British airships over the North Sea in 1918 protects a British convoy from U-boat attack.

could carry a bomb weighing 2,200 pounds (998 kilograms), and terrorized Britain until 1916. By that time the British had developed the giant Handley-Page 0/400 bomber, with twin Rolls Royce engines and a range of over 200 miles (321 kilometers), which attacked German towns night and day in 1917.

Germany also built the first fighter planes. The Dutch designer, Anthony Fokker, built the E-type monoplane fighter for Germany during the first years of the war. It was an agile, strong plane that devastated the Allied forces' heavy, slow observation planes, and for the next year and a half, the Allied planes endured what became known as the "Fokker Scourge." But, by 1917, the Allied forces began to challenge the Fokker, and the jousting match in the air became more evenly matched.

The air war turned young fighter pilots, many of whom did not know how to fly before they enlisted, into heroes called flying aces. The greatest ace of the war was Baron Manfred von Richtofen, who shot down eighty enemy planes before his death in 1918 at the age of twenty-six. The British

Above: This plane is a replica of the Fokker Dr.I, one of the planes that Germany's leading air ace, Baron Manfred von Richtofen, known as the "Red Baron," flew during World War I.

Opposite: British Lieutenant Warneford earned the gratitude of his countrymen when he singlehandedly shot down a German Zeppelin from the skies over Great Britain.

Above: Von Richtofen's squadron, the Flying Circus, is lined up and ready to fly at an airfield during World War I. Von Richtofen's *Albatros* is the second plane from the front.

Right: Lothar von Richtofen (left) stands beside his older brother, Manfred. Both wear the Prussian Blue Max on their collars, Imperial Germany's highest medal for bravery.

called him the "Red Baron," for the bright red Albatross and the Fokker Dr.1 Triplane he flew. Von Richtofen's squadron, known as the Flying Circus, was one of the most deadly in the skies, with superior fighting tactics and planes that obliged the Allied forces to constantly develop better fighters.

The United States entered the war in the summer of 1917 with less training and fewer planes than the Europeans had had in 1914. Some American enlisted men trained in Texas with the dependable Curtiss JN-4 biplane—called the Jenny—before being shipped abroad, but most learned to fly in France. The Americans' greatest contribution to the air war came in the last months, when fifteen hundred allied planes, under the command of American General Billy Mitchell, wrested control of the air from the Germans at St. Mihiel, France, during the first large air campaign in history.

After the war ended, the governments of the Allied forces sold their surplus aircraft at rock bottom prices. Pilots and mechanics who served in the war were also out of jobs. Teams of veteran pilots and mechanics found work entertaining crowds across the United States in the old Curtiss Jenny trainers. This phenomenon was called barnstorming, named after the traveling theater companies in the United States who slept in barns. Barnstormers staged dogfights, and took passengers up for joy rides for a few dollars. Barnstorming remained popular around

Above: France's World War I flying ace Charles Nungesser wears his battle scars and military honors with pride. He disappeared over the Atlantic Ocean the day before Charles Lindbergh left on his triumphant transatlantic flight in May of 1929.

Left: In the early months of the First World War, targets were bombed by air for the first time. In September 1914, British pilots dropped bombs by hand over the Zeppelin sheds in Dusseldorf, Germany.

Right: Airship commander Peter Strasser (right) surveys the horizon in the gondola of the German airship *L.6* in 1915. The *L.6* attempted unsuccessfully to bomb the English coast in January of that year.

Right: Germany used hot air balloons for reconnaissance during the First World War. Observers often had to parachute to safety when Allied pilots shot the balloons down.

the world until the 1930s, and, like the air shows, introduced thousands of people to flying.

The early days of aviation ended in 1919, when Britain and the United States made two pioneering flights across the Atlantic. In May, three Navy Curtiss NC-4 flying boats attempted to fly from Newfoundland to Britain via the Azores in the Atlantic. Only one of the Nancys made the trip, and it took fifteen days. This was the first air crossing from North America to Europe, but it was not non-stop.

One month after the Curtiss flying boat arrived in Britain, a team of British aviators, Captain John Alcock and Lieutenant Arthur Whitten-Brown, flew their converted Vickers Vimy bomber non-stop across the Atlantic Ocean, collecting the £10,000 prize the London newspaper, *The Daily Mail*, had offered to the pilots of the first non-stop Atlantic crossing.

Right: J. P. Williamson lied about his age to join the United States Army in 1918. The seventeen year-old soon learned to fly, and rose to become Chairman of the South Carolina Aeronautics Commission.

Chapter Two

ℬLAZING THE TRAILS

etween the world wars, pilots opened up the air routes and started the international network of airways in use today. The 1920s saw the most famous of these trailblazing flights, when, spurred on by prize money, the promise of fame, and the challenge to be the first to fly a route, pilots made one spectacular trip after another.

THE GREAT AUSTRALIAN AIR RACE

Only two months after Alcock and Brown flew 1,800 miles (2,896 kilometers) across the Atlantic, a crew of Australians, also in a Vimy, set off on a flight more than six times as long from London to Australia. Led by pilot Captain Ross Smith, they were after the prize the Australian government was giving to the first pilot to link England with Australia in less than thirty days; today that prize would be worth half a million dollars.

The 11,000 mile (17,700 kilometer) flight was so difficult that it is hard to believe anyone would have undertaken it in 1919, much less succeeded—but Ross Smith was the perfect person for the job. He had flown for Lawrence of Arabia during the 1918 campaign against the Turks in the Middle East in the First World War, and had previously covered much of the route to Australia during this time, as well as in his post-war work flying survey flights—flights that seek out the best air routes—for the British government from Egypt to India.

Captain Smith's brother, Keith Smith, accompanied him on the race to Australia, navigating with only the help of a compass and land maps while mechanics Jim Bennet and Wally Shiers kept the twin-engined Vimy running. The

Opposite: American actor Reed Howes jumps from an airborne plane to a moving car for a 1928 film. This was one of the most popular stunts at air shows before the Second World War.

Below: Captain Ross Smith and his crew inspect their Vickers Vimy bomber in the summer of 1919 before the start of the 11,000-mile (17,700-kilometer) air race from London to Australia.

France et Colonies. 3 fr. »»
Étranger.. .. .. .. 3 fr. 50

Nº 64. — Sept. 1922

LA SCIENCE ET LA VIE

Left: The cover of this French science magazine from 1922 shows an experimental American helicopter. Helicopters developed more slowly than airplanes, and in 1924 the world helicopter record for distance was only half a mile (.8 of a kilometer).

Opposite top: Spectators at Lympne in Great Britain congratulate Owen Cathcart Jones and Kenneth Waller. On November 2, 1934 the pilots came in fourth place in the London to Melbourne round trip race in their D.H. Comet.

Opposite below: Flying in the *Southern Cross*, Australian aviator Charles Kingsford-Smith and Charles Ulm arrived in the Hawaiian Islands on June 1, 1928, after leaving San Francisco the day before. When they reached Sydney, Australia nine days later, they became the first men to cross the Pacific Ocean by air.

members of the crew were all veterans of the First World War, and when they left London in July of 1919 bound for Australia they were heading home.

The crew of the Vimy had to overcome a series of obstacles and near disasters in the air and on the ground before they arrived safely in Australia twenty-eight days later. The Smith brothers' triumphant flight awakened the world to the power of the airplane to reach even the remotest places, and many other aviators followed their lead, blazing new long-distance air routes. Passengers would not travel most of these routes for years, yet already a number of ambitious aviators and business people were creating the first airlines.

WICKER CHAIRS
AND HAUTE CUISINE

On August 25, 1919, a British company called Aircraft Transport and Travel began the world's first international passenger air service. On that date, four passengers accompanied pilot Major Cyril Patterson in a de Havilland D.H.16 from London to Paris at 12:40 PM. The noise and vibration in the cabin of the converted bomber was so loud that people had to scream to be heard.

All the major European countries founded airlines soon after the war ended, and they established an extensive network of air routes across Europe. But the London to Paris route was the most glamorous of all. From the mid-1920s, Britain's Imperial Airways and France's Air Union provided full gourmet meals to passengers on the popular lunchtime route.

Above: In 1923, the Curtiss CR-3 seaplane won the Schneider Trophy, the most prestigious air race of its time. This was the first American entry to win the contest that began in Monaco in 1913.

Left: In World War I, seaplanes like Great Britain's Short 320 operated from warships and performed reconnaissance in addition to dropping torpedoes on enemy targets.

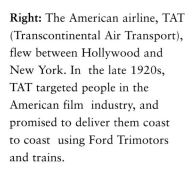

Above: The Glester-Napier VI defended the Schneider Trophy for Great Britain in 1929. Great Britain won the trophy outright in 1931.

Right: The American airline, TAT (Transcontinental Air Transport), flew between Hollywood and New York. In the late 1920s, TAT targeted people in the American film industry, and promised to deliver them coast to coast using Ford Trimotors and trains.

THE
JACQUES SCHNEIDER
MARITIME TROPHY
_____"_____
Presented in 1912 to the
AÉRO CLUB DE FRANCE
by M. Jacques Schneider for an
International Aviation
Competition under Rules
approved by the Federation
Aeronautique Internationale

GREAT BRITAIN
· HOLDER ·
Nº OF WINS: 3
YEARS: 1914, 1922, 1927.

U. S. A.
Nº OF WINS: 2
YEARS: 1923, 1925.

ITALY
RUNNER-UP
Nº OF WINS: 3
YEARS: 1920, 1921, 1926.

FRANCE
Nº OF WINS: 1
YEAR: 1913.

There was plenty of time for lunch; the flight, which covered 200 miles (322 kilometers), took anywhere from two to four hours, depending on the weather over the English Channel.

Many of the passenger airplanes in the 1920s were designed to make their mostly wealthy customers feel like they were traveling on a luxury train. Closed cabins featured wicker chairs, fringed curtains on the windows, and even vases of fresh flowers. The pilots, however, flew in much less comfort. They felt more able to judge shifts in the weather when they were in an open cockpit, and in the days before radio, they often needed to navigate by following landmarks on the ground such as railroad tracks.

Right: This 1921 French guide to air travel on the popular London to Paris route was published two years after the route began in London.

Overleaf: A passenger in an American two-seater biplane in the 1920s goes temporarily insane and attacks the pilot. Many people in the early days of aviation believed flying could drive people mad.

The world's first mid-air collision occurred on the London to Paris route in 1922. The pilots of a French Farman Goliath and a British D.H.18 were traveling in opposite directions, while following the same side of a road down below. In bad weather over northern France the two planes met each other head on, and everyone was killed in the ensuing crash.

Using flying boats, Italian and French airlines established air service across the Mediterranean Sea in the early 1920s. Alla Littoria, an Italian airline, worked a service between Italy and Tunis and Tripoli in North Africa and Haifa in what is now Israel. The French airline, Aeropostale, the

forerunner of Air France, opened service between Marseilles and Algiers in the French colony of Algeria in 1923, using twin-engined, four-passenger flying boats.

The most advanced single-engined light passenger planes in the world for much of the 1920s were the metal monoplanes designed by Germany's Hugo Junkers and Anthony Fokker from the Netherlands, who also designed the first planes specifically for passenger transport: the Junkers F13 and the Fokker FII and FIII.

The Junkers F13 was one of the most successful passenger planes of the

Above: Woman aviator Keith Miller discovers a snake onboard her Avro Avian biplane during the Burmese portion of her London–Australia flight in 1928.

Overleaf top: Daredevils Ivan Unger and Gladys Roy play tennis on the wing of an airborne Curtiss JN "Jenny" in 1925.

Left: Deutsche Luft Hansa began regular passenger service seven years after the London–Paris route began. This Dornier Komet III first flew from Berlin to Zurich on April 6, 1926.

Below: American Admiral Richard Byrd accepts a bag of mail before the start of his second polar flight. Glamorous publicity like this helped convince Americans to use air mail.

1920s. The single-engined monoplane was powered by a BMW 184-horsepower engine, and accommodated four passengers in a comfortable cabin; it was the first plane to have seatbelts. Junkers introduced the corrugated aluminum skin on the F13, which was to become his trademark. A total of 322 F13s were built from 1919 to 1932; the small plane helped many European airlines get started, and serviced Luft Hansa's domestic routes until 1938.

Although all the countries in Europe provided regular passenger service in the 1920s, some Europeans took to the air with more enthusiasm than others. Luft Hansa flew one million passengers from 1919 to 1934, ten times as many as any other European airline during that time. For those airlines whose passenger programs were not as popular as Luft Hansa's, state sponsorship helped keep some European airlines alive. In 1929, ticket sales provided French airlines with only ten per cent of their income; the balance came from air mail and government subsidies.

AIR MAIL

Europeans pioneered air mail flights as well as passenger transport. In 1911, a British Captain, Walter Windham, became the first air mail pilot when he flew letters in Allahabad, India as a publicity stunt to raise money for a local charity. Windham inaugurated air mail service in Britain later that year when he organized air mail flights in London in honor of King George V's coronation.

Almost all European airlines flew mail along with passengers throughout the 1920s and 1930s, and counted on the air mail to get them through their first decade. But the air mail played an even greater role in the United States, where passenger airlines developed in fits and starts, and, until the late 1920s, contracts with the United States Post Office were more profitable than flying passengers.

Mail service by air began in the United States May 15, 1918, when army pilots flew Curtiss JN-4 biplanes between Washington, Philadelphia, and New York. The Jenny was a good trainer, but not adequate for flying air mail. When the Post Office took over the mail service in August of that year, it purchased more than one hundred American-built army war surplus D.H.4Bs. These open-cockpit biplanes formed the bulk of the Post Office's fleet for many years.

Flying mail for the Post Office was so lucrative that one of the first passenger airlines in the United States, Aeromarine Airways, actually gave up a successful passenger business when the Post Office granted it an air mail route in 1924. During the first years of its operation, the United States

Above: The *Graf Zeppelin* glides over Manhattan in 1929. Airship commander Hugo Eckener agreed to officially begin the *Graf*'s round-the-world flight from nearby Lakehurst, New Jersey to please the American promoter of the flight, William Randolph Hearst.

Opposite below: Stuntman Schlindler floats over the cockpit of a two-seater plane in the 1920s. He died when this plane collided with the one he was attempting to change to.

Above: Charles Lindbergh taxis to a landing at Mitchell Field on New York's Long Island in October of 1927. He was completing his aerial tour of the then forty-eight American states five months after his non-stop solo flight across the Atlantic.

government still considered air mail an experiment. Air mail pilots, many of them veterans, established service from the East Coast to Omaha, Nebraska, cutting days off the time mail traveled by train. Yet despite that tremendous accomplishment, President Warren Harding considered discontinuing air mail service in 1921.

The Post Office decided to stage a dramatic non-stop relay from coast to coast to gain support for the service. On February 22, 1921, two air mail planes took off from Long Island and headed west, while another two planes headed east from San Francisco toward the halfway point in Omaha.

The rally did not go as planned, however. One of the eastbound planes crashed and the pilot was killed. Another pilot, Jack Knight, became a hero when he flew his D.H.4 700 miles (1,126 kilometers)—many of them following railroad tracks and bonfires set by local inhabitants during a nighttime snowstorm.

The mail reached New York from San Francisco in thirty-three hours, instead of the 108 it had taken using trains at night. President Harding agreed to support the Post Office's request to light the transcontinental airway. In 1924 the government installed beacons along the route, and the Post Office scheduled air mail flights around the clock.

AIR MAIL PASSENGERS

Passenger travel in the United States got a boost when a bill designed to stimulate commercial aviation passed Congress in 1925. According to the terms of the Kelly Bill, the government allowed passengers to ride

on regularly scheduled mail routes. Most airlines continued to ignore passengers altogether, however, or used them as fill in on slow mail days.

One of the earliest passenger lines to operate after the Kelly Bill, Varney Airlines began to run open-cockpit biplanes between Pasco in Washington State and Elko, Nevada via Boise, Idaho. Varney made passengers sign an agreement saying they would get off at any point during the route if the pilot had to take on more mail. Almost every large American airline got their start in the mid-1920s flying the air mail like Varney, which eventually merged with other airlines to become United Air Lines, one of the largest airlines in the United States today.

After American aviator and air mail pilot Charles Lindbergh flew his historic non-stop solo flight from New York to Paris in 1927, air travel suddenly became glamorous. One airline, Transcontinental Air Transport (TAT) hoped to cash in on that glamour, and began a service from Hollywood, California to New York. TAT hired Lindbergh and Amelia Earhart, the famous American aviator, to fly on the airline's first flight from California across the country, boasting that using a combination of air service by day and rail service by night, passengers could reach the coast in less than three days.

Despite its star-studded publicity, the cross-country route lost TAT millions of dollars. The western route in the unpressurized cabins of the day was particularly turbulent and uncomfortable. Yet despite TAT's early misfortune, the airline merged with Western Air Express in 1931 to form Transcontinental and Western Air (TWA).

Above: A 1938 postcard of the LZ130, the *Graf Zeppelin II*. The German government used the airship to spy on Great Britain on the eve of World War II.

Overleaf: On May 22, 1927 *The New York Times* devoted its entire front page to Charles Lindbergh's successful solo flight from New York to Paris.

Section 1 | "All the News That's Fit to Print." | **The New York Times.** | THE WEATHER Generally fair today and tomorrow; moderate to fresh southerly winds. Temperature yesterday—Max., 56; Min., 53. **☞** For weather report see Page 21. | Section 1

VOL. LXXVI....No. 25,320. **••••** | NEW YORK, SUNDAY, MAY 22, 1927. | *Including Rotogravure Picture Section in three sections* *Magazine and Book Sections in Rotogravure* FIVE CENTS In Manhattan Bronx and Brooklyn TEN CENTS Elsewhere

LINDBERGH DOES IT! TO PARIS IN 33½ HOURS; FLIES 1,000 MILES THROUGH SNOW AND SLEET; CHEERING FRENCH CARRY HIM OFF FIELD

COULD HAVE GONE 500 MILES FARTHER

Gasoline for at Least That Much More— Flew at Times From 10 Feet to 10,000 Feet Above Water

ATE ONLY ONE AND A HALF OF HIS FIVE SANDWICHES

Fell Asleep at Times but Quickly Awoke—Glimpses of His Adventure in Brief Interview at the Embassy.

LINDBERGH'S OWN STORY TOMORROW.

Captain Charles A. Lindbergh was too exhausted after his arrival in Paris late last night to do more than indicate, as told below, his experiences during his flight. After he awakes today, he will narrate the full story of his remarkable exploit for readers of Monday's New York Times.

By CARLYLE MACDONALD.

Copyright, 1927, by The New York Times Company. *Special Cable to THE NEW YORK TIMES.*

PARIS, Sunday, May 22.—Captain Lindbergh was discovered at the American Embassy at 2:30 o'clock this morning. Attired in a pair of Ambassador Herrick's pajamas, he sat on the edge of a bed and talked of his flight. At the last moment Ambassador Herrick had canceled the plans of the reception committee and, by unanimous consent, took the flier to the embassy in the Place d'Iena.

A staff of American doctors who had arrived at Le Bourget Field early to minister to an "exhausted" aviator found instead a bright-eyed, smiling youth who refused to be examined.

"Oh, don't bother; I am all right," he said.

"I'd like to have a bath and a glass of milk. I would feel better," Lindbergh replied when the Ambassador asked him what he would like to have.

A bath was drawn immediately and in less than five minutes the youth had disrobed in one of the embassy guest rooms, taken his bath and was out again drinking a bottle of milk and eating a roll.

"No Use Worrying," He Tells Envoy.

"There is no use worrying about me, Mr. Ambassador," Lindbergh insisted when Mr. Herrick and members of the embassy staff wanted him to be examined by doctors and then go to bed immediately.

It was apparent that the young man was too full of his experiences to want sleep and he sat on the bed and chatted with the Ambassador, his son and daughter-in-law.

By this time a corps of frantic newspaper men who had been madly chasing the airman, following one false scent after another, had finally tracked him to the embassy. In a body they descended upon the Ambassador, who received them in the salon and informed them that he had just left Lindbergh with strict instructions to go to sleep.

Expected Trouble Over Newfoundland.

In the blue and gold room, with a soft light glowing, sat the conqueror of the Atlantic. He immediately stood up and held out his hands to greet his callers. THE NEW YORK TIMES correspondent being first to greet him.

"Sit down, please," urged every one with one voice, but Lindbergh only smiled again his famous boyish smile and said: "It's almost as easy to stand up as it is to sit down."

Questions were fired at him from all sides about his trip across the ocean, but Lindbergh seemed to dismiss them all with brief, nonchalant answers.

"I expected trouble over Newfoundland because I had been warned that the situation there was unfavorable. But I got over that hazard with no trouble whatsoever."

Sleet and Snow for 1,000 Miles.

"However, it wasn't easy going. I had sleet and snow for over 1,000 miles. Sometimes it was too high to fly over and sometimes too low to fly under, so I just had to go through it as best I could.

"I flew as low as 10 feet in some places and as high as 10,000 in others. I passed no ships in the daytime, but at night I saw the lights of several ships, the night being bright and clear.

"Everyone then wanted to know if the flier had been sleepy on the voyage.

"I didn't really get what you might call downright sleepy," he said, "but I think I sort of nodded several times. In fact, I could have flown half that distance again. I had enough fuel

Continued on Page Two.

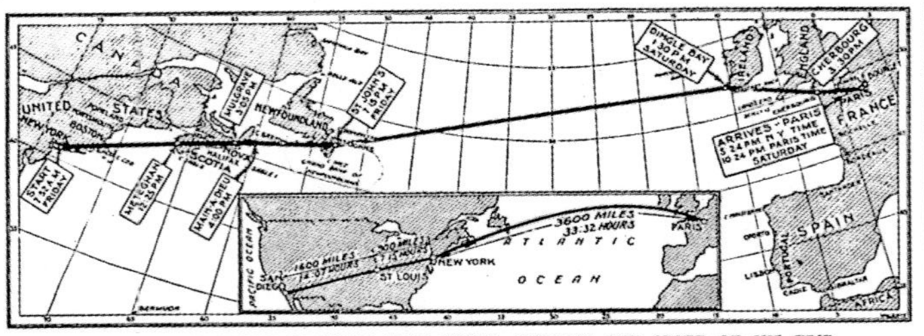

LEVINE ABANDONS BELLANCA FLIGHT

Venture Given Up as Designer Splits With Him—Plane Narrowly Escapes Burning.

BYRD'S CRAFT IS NAMED

Lindbergh Cheered at Ceremony—Commander, Now Last in Field, Waits on Weather.

Through no fault of his own, Clarence D. Chamberlin, who with Bert Acosta established a world's non-stop flying record a few weeks ago, will not fly the record-breaking monoplane in an attempt to establish a second New York-Paris non-stop flight.

G. M. Bellanca, designer of the plane, and Charles S. Levine of the Columbia Aircraft Company, owner of the ship, came to the parting of the ways last night and the designer finally severed his connection with the promoter. Then Levine issued a statement that the proposed flight, which has been talked of for weeks, was off.

The statement said:

"Due to the crowning blow of Mr. Bellanca's resignation, the plane will be placed in the hangar. Mr. Bellanca's resignation causes us to abandon plans for the New York-Paris flight for the present."

At the very moment that the statement was issued the plane was near the runway at Roosevelt Field with gas tanks filled and all equipment aboard ready for the start for Paris.

Plane Threatened by Fire.

A few minutes later, as it was being wheeled off, preparatory to being housed for the night, it narrowly escaped being destroyed by fire. When the word came to the field that the flight was definitely off, mechanics were ordered to empty one gasoline tank to lighten the machine. The gasoline spilled on the ground and while the ship was being towed away a careless spectator threw the stub of a lighted cigarette down.

In an instant there was a terrific flare and a dense burst of smoke as the gasoline blazed up.

"The Bellanca's gone," was the cry that rose from thousands of spectators who had gathered at the field.

Word was flashed to the army air station at Mitchel Field that there had been an accident and ambulances and fire-fighting apparatus were sent across the road. An ambulance from the Nassau County Hospital at Mineola was also sent to Roosevelt Field, as well as fire apparatus from Mineola.

The flames, however, was beyond the danger line and was not injured.

It had been announced that the Columbia would take off at 8 o'clock and Chamberlin was in his flying clothes ready to climb into the cockpit with the unnamed pilot who was to have accompanied him on the trip.

With the elimination of the Bellanca monoplane, only Lieut.

Continued on Page Four.

MAP OF LINDBERGH'S TRANSATLANTIC ROUTE, SHOWING THE SPEED OF HIS TRIP.

CAPTAIN CHARLES A. LINDBERGH, Who Flew Alone Across the Atlantic, New York to Paris, in Thirty-three and One-half Hours.

Times Wide World Photo

New York Stages Big Celebration After Hours of Anxious Waiting

Harbor Craft, Factories, Fire Sirens and Radio Carry Message of the Flier's Victory Throughout the City—Theatres Halt While Audiences Cheer.

New York bubbled all day yesterday with excitement and expectancy, first yearning for word of Captain Lindbergh, then half-doubting, gaining confidence as the afternoon progressed and finally acclaiming the victory of the young aviator with street demonstrations where the crowds were thickest, in which the ancient phrase, "I told you so," was often repeated. It was evident during the day that New York had confidence in the lad from the West.

On the streets and elsewhere Lindbergh was the one topic of conversation the whole day long. In the subway, on the elevated, in trains and cars, motion-picture houses, theatres, wherever a few had gathered, or even where one man could find another to talk to, one heard "Lindbergh — Lindbergh — Lindbergh."

And such expressions as this: "He'll make it, all right."

"Some baby!"

"Well, if he's hit Ireland, he's safe anyway."

"He's away ahead of his time."

"What's the difference in time between here and there, anyway?"

Confused On Difference in Time.

To this latter question there were some amazing answers. One woman who had the aviator's running time mixed with the difference in time between New York and Paris solemnly informed her companion that there was thirty-six hours difference in time between the cities.

She said it with an air which signified: "I don't mean maybe." A surprising number of persons insisted that the difference in time was three hours.

Early in the day, even before there was any good reason why there should be definite news, the interest of the people was demonstrated in two ways. At every news stand there were little groups scanning the headlines and buying newspapers. In every newspaper office the switchboards were literally swamped with inquiries. It was not sufficient that the operator said there was no word, or, later, that Lindbergh's plane had been seen over Ireland. The inquirers wanted specific information:

"Well, when will you get the first news?" they asked. And later:

"If he's over Ireland how long will it be before he gets to Paris?"

"Is he all right?"

The questions that were asked, considering that no news could possibly come direct from Captain Lindbergh before he landed, were as surprising as the guesses at the difference in time.

The Times Gets 10,000 Phone Calls.

The telephone inquiries came from all sorts of people and all directions. Not a few rang up THE TIMES office and apologetically explained that they were on golf links or elsewhere at a distance, and hence could not

Continued on Page Three.

LINDBERGH TRIUMPH THRILLS COOLIDGE

President Cables Praise to "Heroic Flier" and Concern for Nungesser and Coli.

CAPITAL THROBS WITH JOY

Kellogg, New, MacNider, Patrick and Many More Join in Paying Tribute to Daring Youth.

Special to The New York Times.

WASHINGTON, May 21.—The triumph of Captain Charles A. Lindbergh in flying from New York to Paris without a stop created a tremendous sensation in the national capital and found immediate response in a host of official messages and statements congratulating the daring aviator upon his achievement.

President Coolidge expressed his admiration in a message transmitted through Ambassador Herrick in Paris for delivery to the young flier in person.

With a single possible exception, this city has never been more thrilled since the armistice, when Woodrow Wilson mingled with many thousands in celebrating the end of the war. The exception was when Walter Johnson arose from apparent defeat and won the deciding world series baseball game in 1924.

"The American people," the President said, "rejoice with me at the brilliant termination of your heroic flight. The first non-stop flight of a lone aviator across the Atlantic crowns the record of American aviation, and in bringing the greetings of the American people to France you likewise carry the assurance of our admiration of those intrepid Frenchmen, Nungesser and Coli, whose bold spirits first ventured on your exploit, and likewise a message of our continued anxiety concerning their fate."

Secretary Kellogg, in a message similarly transmitted, said:

"I heartily congratulate you on the success of your great adventure in accomplishing a non-stop flight from New York to Paris. It is a great step in the advancement of aviation. Every one in the United States is proud of your accomplishment."

Knew Lindbergh as a Boy.

In a statement issued here Mr. Kellogg referred to his personal friendship for Lindbergh, whom he has known for years through the young man's late father, a Representative in Congress from the Secretary's home State of Minnesota.

"News has just reached me," Mr. Kellogg said, "of the success of Lindbergh in completing his flight from New York to Paris. It is an achievement of which every American can justly be proud. I have known Lindbergh since he was a boy and rejoice at this culmination of his ambitions, which could only have been gained by scientific knowledge, superb courage and physique and sterling character. Our rejoicing in Lindbergh's success, however, is tempered by our continued ignorance of the fate of Nungesser and Coli, whose courage and valor have now been equaled, but cannot be surpassed."

Hanford MacNider, Acting Secre-

Continued on Page Four.

CROWD ROARS THUNDEROUS WELCOME

Breaks Through Lines of Soldiers and Police and Surging to Plane Lifts Weary Flier from His Cockpit

AVIATORS SAVE HIM FROM FRENZIED MOB OF 100,000

Paris Boulevards Ring With Celebration After Day and Night Watch—American Flag Is Called For and Wildly Acclaimed.

By EDWIN L. JAMES.

Copyright, 1927, by The New York Times Company. *Special Cable to THE NEW YORK TIMES.*

PARIS, May 21.—Lindbergh did it. Twenty minutes after 10 o'clock tonight suddenly and softly there slipped out of the darkness a gray-white airplane as 25,000 pairs of eyes strained toward it. At 10:24 the Spirit of St. Louis landed and lines of soldiers, ranks of policemen and stout steel fences went down before a mad rush as irresistible as the tides of the ocean.

"Well, I made it," smiled Lindbergh, as the little white monoplane came to a halt in the middle of the field and the first vanguard reached the plane. Lindbergh made a move to jump out. Twenty hands reached for him and lifted him out as if he were a baby. Several thousands in a minute were around the plane. Thousands more broke the barriers of iron rails round the field, cheering wildly.

Lifted From His Cockpit.

As he was lifted to the ground Lindbergh was pale and with his hair unkempt, he looked completely worn out. He had strength enough, however, to smile, and waved his hand to the crowd. Soldiers with fixed bayonets were unable to keep back the crowd.

United States Ambassador Herrick was among the first to welcome and congratulate the flier.

A NEW YORK TIMES man was one of the first to reach the machine after its graceful descent to the field. Those first to arrive at the plane had a picture that will live in their minds for the rest of their lives. His cap off, his famous locks falling in disarray around his eyes, "Lucky Lindy" sat peering out over the rim of the little cockpit of his machine.

Dramatic Scene at the Field.

It was high drama. Picture the scene. Almost if not quite 100,000 people were massed on the east side of Le Bourget air field. Some of them had been there six and seven hours.

Off to the left the giant phare lighthouse of Mount Valerien flashed its guiding light 300 miles into the air. Closer on the left Le Bourget Lighthouse twinkled, and off to the right another giant revolving phare sent its beams high into the heavens.

Big air lights on all sides with enormous electric glares were flooding the landing field. From time to time rockets rose and burst in varied lights over the field.

Seven thirty, the hour announced for the arrival, had come and gone. Then 8 o'clock came, and no Lindbergh; at 9 o'clock the sun had set but then came reports that Lindbergh had been seen over Cork. Then he had been seen over Valentia in Ireland and then over Plymouth.

Suddenly a message spread like lightning, the aviator had been seen over Cherbourg. However, remembering the messages telling of Captain Nungesser's flight, the crowd was skeptical.

"One chance in a thousand!" "Oh, he cannot do it without navigating instruments!" "It's a pity, because he was a brave boy." Pessimism had spread over the great throng by 10 o'clock.

The stars came out and a chill wind blew.

Watchers Are Twice Disappointed.

Suddenly the field lights flooded their glares onto the landing ground and there came the roar of an airplane's motor. The crowd was still, then began a cheer, but two minutes later the landing glares went dark for the searchlight had identified the plane and it was not Captain Lindbergh's.

Stamping their feet in the cold, the crowd waited patiently. It seemed quite apparent that nearly every one was willing to wait all night, hoping against hope.

Suddenly—it was 10:16 exactly—another motor roared over the heads of the crowd. In the sky once again caught a glimpse of a white gray plane, and for an instant heard the sound of one. Then it dimmed, and the idea spread that it was yet another disappointment.

Again landing lights glared and almost by the time they had flooded the field the gray-white plane had lighted on the far side nearly half a mile from the crowd. It seemed to stop almost as it hit the ground, so gently did it land.

And then occurred a scene which almost passed description. Two companies of soldiers with fixed bayonets and the Le Bourget field police, reinforced by Paris agents, had held the crowd in good order. But as the lights showed the plane

---

THE SPIRIT OF ST. LOUIS

In 1926, Charles Lindbergh was a veteran barnstormer and lieutenant in the United States Army Air Service Reserve. That year he was also responsible for laying out the air mail route from St. Louis, Missouri to Chicago. He flew the first air mail flight between the cities in April of 1926, and flew the route regularly until September of 1926.

Flying the airmail was hazardous in the biplanes of the 1920s. Lindbergh ran out of gas twice, once when he was flying in a fog and another time in snow. He could not find a place to land, and had to parachute from his old D.H.4. Yet despite the danger, Lindbergh grew bored, and set his sights on the most coveted prize in aviation at the time, the $25,000 Orteig Prize for the first non-stop flight between New York and Paris.

Lindbergh, backed by a group of businessmen from St. Louis, chose a small company in San Diego, California, called Ryan to produce his plane for the race. Ryan constructed for Lindbergh an enlarged version of its M-2, a high-winged monoplane that flew mail on the west coast.

Lindbergh's plane was powered by a single Wright Whirlwind air-cooled engine, a major advance over earlier and heavier water-cooled engines. The enlarged M2 was basically an overgrown gas tank, for Lindbergh was one of the few contenders in the race who had decided to fly solo. He figured he would need fuel more during the 3,600-mile (5,792-kilometer) trip than a navigator.

Two months after Ryan began work on Lindbergh's plane, the *Spirit of St. Louis* was ready to fly. On May 10, 1927, Lindbergh left San Diego and flew east across the United States. He arrived at Curtiss Field in New York two days later, after a stop in St. Louis, setting a new transcontinental record.

Above: American aviator Charles Lindbergh stands in front of his Ryan monoplane in 1927 at Curtiss Field on Long Island.

Right: American aviator Amelia
Earhart perches above a throng of
spectators on her Lockheed Vega
in a field near Londonderry,
Ireland on May 21, 1932. Earhart
had just become the first woman
to fly across the Atlantic alone.

The day before Lindbergh left San Diego, the French World War One flying ace, Charles Nungesser, and his copilot, François Coli, had disappeared over the Atlantic in the storm system that had stalled Lindbergh's departure from New York for a week. Nungesser and Coli had left Paris on May 8 for New York in Nungesser's single-engined biplane *L'Oiseau Blanc* (*"The White Bird"*).

Ships in the North Atlantic were searching for the missing French aviators when Lindbergh finally took off for Paris on May 20. Lindbergh had already become somewhat of a legend in the United States during his week in New York. The dark horse of the race, he did not have the experience of the other contestants. Yet ordinary people all over the world rooted for the young airmail pilot who was brave enough to fly across the Atlantic alone in a single-engined plane.

Lindbergh arrived in Paris at Le Bourget airfield thirty-three hours after leaving New York and claimed the Orteig Prize. France was still grieving

over the loss of their beloved Nungesser, and they extended the hero's
welcome they had prepared for him to the American aviator.

Back in the United States, Americans greeted Lindbergh like royalty. His
flight across the Atlantic, the most celebrated feat in aviation since the
invention of the airplane, sparked a boom in commercial aviation in the
United States. In the first twelve months after Lindbergh's flight,
applications for pilot licenses in the United States tripled, and the number
of airline passengers quadrupled.

MILESTONES

The 1920s closed with three spectacular flights in three very different
aircraft. On November 28 and 29, 1929, the American Naval Commander,
Richard Byrd, and a crew of three in a Ford Trimotor made the first flight
over the South Pole. Byrd then became the first person to fly over the
North and the South Poles. He and Floyd Bennett, his pilot, flew over the

Above: A ship unloads American explorer and aviator Richard Byrd's Ford Trimotor, the *Floyd Bennett*, onto Antarctic land in 1929. The frozen land collapsed a few hours after this photograph was taken, but no serious damage was done.

Right: The dining room of the *Graf Zeppelin* served airship passengers gourmet meals in an elegant setting.

North Pole in a Fokker Trimotor in 1926. Byrd's polar flights meant that by 1929, no place on earth was out of reach of the airplane.

The land-based airplane was not the only aircraft performing spectacular flights. Germany, was responsible for two landmark flights in two different kinds of aircraft: the Zeppelin and the flying boat. From August 8 to 29, 1929 the *Graf Zeppelin*, Zeppelin's most advanced dirigible ever, flew around the world with twenty passengers and twice as many crew members. No airplane of the day was capable of transporting passengers around the world, much less in the luxury the *Graf Zeppelin* provided. For up to $9,000 apiece, passengers dined on gourmet food and fine wine.

As the German airship was reaching its peak in 1929, the country also produced the largest airplane in the world: the giant Dornier DO-X monoplane flying boat. The DO-X had twelve engines mounted back-to-back, and its wing span was a massive 157 feet (48 meters), 20 feet (6 meters) more than the first turbo jets produced in the 1950s. Its passenger facilities rivaled the *Graf Zeppelin*, with three decks and a 60-foot-long (18-meter) salon for dining and dancing.

The DO-X was not a practical plane. Its epic flight in 1931 from Lake Constance, where Dornier's plant was located, to New York took nine months to complete. But the DO-X proved that giant, multi-engined airplanes were possible, and that the time had come for the large flying boat.

Below: Here is the twelve-engined Dornier in flight. Dornier worked for the Zeppelin Company in Friedrichshafen, Germany, before he built the Do-X in the same town.

Chapter Three

The Battle for the Sky

During the 1930s the Depression that had begun in the United States spread throughout the world, but it could not stop the growth of aviation. Aviators still made spectacular long-distance flights, and Amelia Earhart and Amy Johnson captured the imagination of the world. But the greatest story of the last decade of aviation's Golden Age is how the airplane grew up and won out over the airship.

During the 1920s airships had become so luxurious in the hands of the Germans that they rivaled the great ocean liners crossing the Atlantic. The *Graf Zeppelin* flew passengers to all corners of the globe, even to the North Pole. At the time, most people thought the airship was the long-distance aircraft of the future. No one knew that one of the most spectacular disasters in history would doom the airship to extinction.

In the Arms of Angels

Soon after the *Graf Zeppelin* was launched in 1928, the Zeppelin Company began planning their next great airship. Six years later, on March 4, 1936, the *Hindenburg*, an even larger and more powerful Zeppelin, was finished in Friedrichscafen. At 804 feet (245 meters) in length, only 78 feet (24 feet) shorter than the ill-fated ocean liner, the *Titanic*, the *Hindenburg* was the largest aircraft that ever flew, or has ever flown since.

The *Hindenburg* would make ten scheduled round-trip flights between Germany and the United States, as well as seven non-stop

Opposite: A seaplane approaches a landing on water in this 1928 illustration.

Below: Passengers board an Air France airliner in the 1930s.

flights between Germany and Rio de Janeiro, Brazil, during its first season in 1936; but the great airship first had to accompany the *Graf Zeppelin* on a tour of Germany on behalf of the Nazi party.

The so-called "airship of the German people" was actually not that at all. Like the *Graf Zeppelin*, the *Hindenburg* was reserved for wealthy travelers, and it was even more exclusive than most ocean liners of the time. There were no second class or steerage accommodations; the whole airship was first class. A one way ticket on the *Hindenburg's* Atlantic run cost $400, the price of a car at the time, but that was a bargain compared to a first class ticket on the *Queen Mary*, the most luxurious ocean liner on the transatlantic route.

The passengers who were lucky enough to fly on the *Hindenburg* experienced the most elegant, comfortable travel ever. Up to fifty people

Opposite top: The German airship *Hindenburg* lands at the Zeppelin landing field in Frankfurt after a record-breaking forty-eight-hour flight in the 1930s.

Opposite below: This aerial photograph shows the charred remains of the *R101*, a British airship which crashed into a hillside in Beauvais, France on October 5, 1930 en route to India during its first voyage.

were housed in the style and comfort of a grand hotel. They were served gourmet meals at tables draped in white linen and set with silver and china created just for the airship, dining on venison and roast duckling and sipping fine wine, while they viewed the changing skyscape below.

The *Hindenburg* cruised along at 80 miles per hour (128 kilometers), but so smoothly that people barely felt the ship moving. Passengers played a game to see how long a pen or pencil could be stood on end without falling over, and most people tired of waiting. Even when the *Hindenburg* passed through rain, hail, and rough winds, the giant ship just rolled gently.

Ocean liners could not compete with the smoothness and quiet of the *Hindenburg*, and in fact, no other craft has ever come close. Louis P. Lochner, a prominent newsman on one of the *Hindenburg*'s flights, was allowed to visit the so-called "seaman's rest," a perch in the bow of the ship where almost no engine vibration was felt. The newcomer to airship travel confided in his diary that, "You feel as though you were carried in the arms of angels."

THE *HINDENBURG* DISASTER

In the 1920s and 1930s, Britain and the United States had each launched ambitious airship programs, but unlike the Zeppelin Company, which maintained a near-perfect safety record, they were plagued by disaster, and by 1935 they were out of business. So it was that on May 3, 1937, when the *Hindenburg* was ready to begin a new season of its popular transatlantic passenger service, the Zeppelin Company was the last bastion of the airship.

When the *Hindenburg* left its new station in Frankfurt on May 3, 1937 for a two-day flight across the North Atlantic, the airship seemed

invincible. The crossing over the Atlantic was uneventful for the passengers, but Captain Max Pruss battled strong headwinds. The ship arrived in Manhattan, thirty minutes from the Naval base in Lakehurst, New Jersey, almost half a day behind schedule.

While the captain waited for a line of thunderstorms to clear over Lakehurst, he treated passengers to a close-up view of Manhattan, flying the *Hindenburg* over the Empire State Building, the tallest building in the world when it was built in 1931. The airship sailed low enough so that passengers could wave to the tourists on the building's observation deck, and see photographers taking pictures of them.

In a light rain on the evening of May 6, the *Hindenburg* received a radio communication from Lakehurst that the weather was clearing. The airship arrived, and the crew began the mooring procedure. They valved off hydrogen gas in the various gas cells on the airship to lower the ship's altitude and trim it so the landing would be on an even keel. They also released the water from ballast bags in the rear, to level the ship.

As the 231 crewmen on the ground prepared to guide the airship to the mooring mast with the ship's handling lines, with the *Hindenburg* hovering about 300 feet (91 meters) above the ground, fire suddenly appeared near the ship's tail. Within less than 30 seconds the ship was engulfed in flames, and the only passengers who got out alive had to jump from the burning ship as it fell to the ground.

Sixty-two out of ninety-seven people on board lived to tell the story of the *Hindenburg* disaster. And thanks to the number of journalists and photographers at the scene, it became the first air disaster in history to be recorded in detail.

Above: Great Britain's Air Minister, Lord Londonderry, and Postmaster General Sir Kingsley Wood inaugurate the England–Australia air mail service on December 8, 1934. The ceremony took place in front of an Imperial Airways H.P. 42 at London's Croydon Airfield.

Above: A United Air Lines DC-3 in flight in the 1930s. The efficient American plane helped make airlines profitable around the world.

Right: In 1938, United Air Lines operated a sky lounge on some of its DC-3s. The cabin accommodated fourteen passengers, and the roomy upholstered seats swiveled toward or away from the windows.

Left: In the spirit of the time, the copy that accompanies this publicity photograph from the 1930s reads: "The cabins of TWA's big Douglas luxury liners are so roomy that a game of bridge may be essayed with complete comfort and ease during flight."

Below: This illustration shows the variety of airplanes that shared the skies from 1919 to 1935. The seaplane, the fastest aircraft at the time, is at the center of the picture.

To this day the cause remains a mystery. Some think it was sabotage, but experts at the time claimed that static electricity ignited the flammable hydrogen gas. But whatever had actually caused the fire, the disaster ended the Zeppelin empire. By 1938 the rigid airship that ruled long-distance air travel for almost twenty years was extinct.

THE GREAT FLYING BOATS

Years before the *Hindenburg's* first voyage, another type of luxury passenger aircraft, the giant flying boat, was taking shape in the United States and Britain. The land-based plane was not capable of carrying passengers on long sectors over water at the time. So the American airline, Pan American, and the British airline, Imperial Airways, developed a series of deluxe four-engined flying boats in the 1930s, which they used to expand their air routes around the world.

The first plane in Pan American's so-called Clipper Ship fleet was the Sikorsky S-40. The S-40, called the *Southern Clipper*, was a luxury liner. It had walnut-paneled walls, heavy silk drapery, and upholstered seats. The *Southern Clipper* carried mail and up to thirty-two passengers on the Miami–Rio de Janeiro route until the more advanced version, the S-42, was launched in 1934. The S-42 cruised at 170 miles per hour (274 kilometers), and had a

Above: The French Nieuport 62 fighter plane of 1931 was a later version of the Nieuport 16 and 17.

Below: American aviator Wiley Post's Lockheed Vega *Winnie Mae* lies nose-first in a field in Alaska. This picture was taken in the middle of his second around-the-world flight in 1933.

range of 1,200 miles (1,930 kilometers).

In 1936, Pan American introduced its Martin M-130 China Clipper flying boats. The China Clippers inaugurated the airline's Pacific flights from California to Manila in the Philippines that year. The huge aircraft had room for eighteen passengers in sleeper cabins, and thirty-two passengers for daytime travel. Its range was almost three times as great as its predecessor, the S-42.

The political connections of Juan Trippe, the founder of Pan American, in Washington played an important part in establishing the Pacific route. Trippe convinced President Roosevelt to let the China Clippers

Right: Douglas Corrigan, a pilot and airplane mechanic, earned the nickname "Wrong Way" Corrigan when he supposedly got lost and flew an unauthorized flight from New York to Ireland in 1938. His flight plan said he was headed to California.

Previous page: This fine watercolor illustrates the French Navy of 1928 and the future to come, as an airplane prepares to land on the aircraft carrier *Bearn* while a submarine glides alongside.

Opposite: Edith Scott completed this portrait of Amelia Earhart in 1932, the year she became the first woman to fly solo across the Atlantic.

rest and refuel on American territories such as Midway Island and Wake Island, in return for establishing bases there. The bases Pan American laid down on these small islands, with facilities for fueling and servicing its flying boats, served Americans well when they entered the air war in the Pacific a few years later.

The last of the clipper series, and the largest, the famous double-decked Boeing 314 Clipper, served on both Pan American's Atlantic and Pacific run.

Right: The "bird man," American Clem Sohn, demonstrates his suit of wings to spectators at Great Britain's Hanworth Air Park in 1936. He jumped from a plane at 10,000 feet (3,050 meters), but it was his parachute, not his wings, that saved him.

Below: A British Hawker Fury in flight. The plane was developed during the two world wars, and represented a cross between the old wood and steel frame covered in fabric, and the new type of metal construction.

The airline's transatlantic service began with the Boeing 314s from Port Washington, Long Island, a few hours outside New York City in 1939.

In Britain, the Short flying boat of 1926 (called the *Singapore*) was the forerunner of Imperial Airways' luxurious double-decked Empire service of the late 1930s. The Short C-class Empire Boats gave Britain a lead on the civil air routes of the world in the 1930s. By 1938, Imperial operated seven services a week to Egypt, four to India, three to East Africa, and two each to South Africa, Malaya, and Australia.

The Empire Boats carried up to twenty-four passengers, and two tons of mail and freight. Passengers loved the spacious cabins and the first class service with white-gloved stewards, even though overnight rest stops on these long trips could be uncomfortable. Layovers on a single route might vary from deluxe accommodations such as the Raffles Hotel in Singapore to a cot in a tent in the Iraqi desert.

THE MODERN AIRLINER

By 1930, Americans were taking to the air in record numbers. That year, American airlines carried 170,000 passengers, nearly twice the number of any other country. All the major airlines in the United States at the time— TWA, Northwest, American, United, Eastern, and Pan American—used Ford Trimotors. The Ford Trimotor, nicknamed the *Tin Goose*, was a strong, reliable plane built by auto-maker Henry Ford, featuring the corrugated aluminum skin pioneered by Junkers.

One of the best civil airplanes in Europe at the time was Junkers Ju52.

Above: One of the 35,000 Messerschmitt 109 fighter planes Germany produced during World War II is shown here in flight. The ace some consider to have been the best pilot of that war, Hans-Joachim Marseille, shot down 158 Allied planes in a Me109.

Overleaf left: In this illustration from a 1938 Italian magazine, residents of Madrid during the Spanish Civil War fear that planes overhead are dropping bombs. But here the bombers are dropping food, not bombs.

Overleaf right: European nations used the Spanish Civil War to test their new fighter aircraft. In this drawing from 1938 Italian bombers are destroying Spanish Republican planes near Valencia.

Above: The German Nazi party financed the construction of the airship *Hindenburg*, in 1936. In return, the airship had to appear at military rallies such as this one at the Nuremburg Zeppelin Field.

Right: The destruction airplanes brought to Madrid during the Spanish Civil War in 1938 spread throughout Europe in World War II.

The three-motored plane was covered in the corrugated sheet duraluminum Junkers made famous, and carried seventeen passengers. It was one of the most rugged airplanes ever built. Junkers sold Ju52s to over thirty different airlines, and the so-called "Iron Annie" became Germany's leading transport of the Second World War.

The Trimotor stayed in service in the United States until 1933 when Ford stopped his airplane production altogether, and the new twin-engined Boeing 247 and the DC-3 took its place. This next generation of airliners was so revolutionary that they made all previous planes, including the Trimotor and the JU52, obsolete.

The airliner of today was born when the American company Boeing introduced its all-metal, twin-engined monoplane on February 8, 1933. It is amazing how modern the Boeing 247 appears. All the elements were designed to be streamlined to reduce the aircraft's resistance to wind and to increase its speed. The retractable landing gear, the single fin and rudder,

Above: This illustration from 1935 shows a BTW Transport seaplane moored in the water. These giant flying craft were designed to look like boats, which is why the windows of the plane are round, like portholes.

Above: The United States Army and Navy flew the Grumman G-21A in World War II. The so-called "Goose" was an amphibian plane that could take off and land on water or dry land.

Right: The Douglas DC-3 *Legend Aviation* at a fiftieth-anniversary celebration of the end of World War II. The DC-3 transport plane, manufactured in Europe and the United States during the war, carried Allied troops, supplies, and civilians.

the smooth, all-metal surface, the low cantilevered wing, and especially the long, teardrop shape of the fuselage all contributed to make the Boeing 247 a beautiful and efficient aircraft.

The Boeing 247, and the Douglas DC series of planes that came after it, created the look and feel adopted by passenger planes all over the world. That sleek, streamlined look was not only a popular style, it was also the most efficient design for passenger transport.

The DC-3 made passenger airlines profitable without air mail for the first time. It began service in June of 1936 on American Airlines New York–Chicago run, carrying twenty-one passengers on its daytime service, and fourteen in its sleeper berths at night. Powered by two 1,200-horsepower Pratt and Whitney Twin Wasp engines, the best aircraft engine of the day, the DC-3 cut the time on the transcontinental run from twenty to sixteen hours, half the time the trip had taken only six years earlier.

By 1939 DC-3s were transporting 90 percent of the world's airline passengers. Over eleven thousand were built for civilian and military use. The DC-3 established the United States as the world leader in commercial aviation, a lead it still has today. It also signaled the land-based airplane's superiority over the flying boat.

Below: This 1936 watercolor shows an Air France Breuguet flying boat and her crew. The French airline used the multi-engined plane on flights across the Mediterranean Sea and along the coast of Africa.

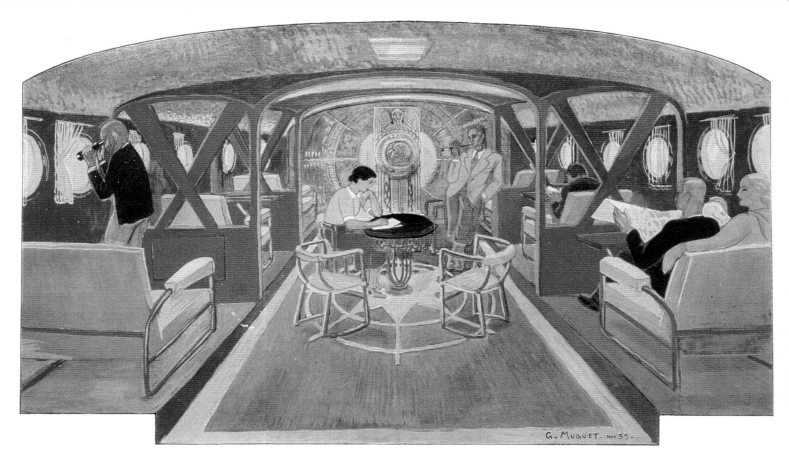

Above: The interior of a flying boat from the 1930s gives a sense of the roominess and luxury enjoyed by passengers. The aircraft were slow, though, and could not compete with the newer, more powerful land-based airplanes after the Second World War.

AROUND THE WORLD

One of the few people in the early 1930s who knew that the airplane would eventually outperform the airship was a one-eyed freelance aviator from Oklahoma named Wiley Post. Post understood that the essence of air travel was speed. Airships had a tremendously long range, but they were slow.

In 1931, Post set out from Roosevelt Field in New York with a navigator in a fast, single-engined Lockheed Vega named the *Winnie Mae*. They flew around the world in eight days, fifteen hours, and fifty-one minutes—beating the *Graf Zeppelin*'s record by more than twelve days.

Two years later Post made another record flight around the world, this time alone in a renovated Winnie Mae. The plane carried the prototype for the Sperry Gyroscope Company's new autopilot flying system, and a radio receiver the United States Army had perfected as an automatic direction finder.

Post left Floyd Bennett Field on Long Island, New York, site of the world's longest concrete runway when the airport opened in 1931, on July 15, 1933. Navigating mostly by dead reckoning, and using the autopilot to save him many hours of tiring manual flying, Post arrived at Berlin's Templehof Airport less than twenty-six hours later. He beat his own world record by two days, and became the first person to fly nonstop from New York to Berlin. But more importantly, his flight proved that navigational and automatic pilot instruments would be standard on airplanes in the future, and that they would revolutionize the airplane's performance.

Another famous aviator on the around the world circuit of the 1930s, Amelia Earhart, is as well-known for her mysterious death as her record-setting flights. Earhart was almost as popular with the American people as Lindbergh. She even resembled the tall, thin, boyish hero so much that her promoters dubbed her the "Lady Lindy."

Although some people who knew Earhart said she was a more courageous pilot than a skilled one, Earhart proved her abilities by setting one record after another. Her fifteen-hour flight across the Atlantic on May 20, 1932 in her Lockheed Vega set three records alone: The fastest crossing of the North Atlantic, the first transatlantic flight piloted by a woman, and the first solo crossing by a woman.

When Earhart set off on what would become her last flight in 1937, a flight around the equator, with her navigator Fred Noonan, she did not intend to set any records for speed. She was doing research at Purdue University in Indiana at the time on the effects of altitude on people, and how to make flying safer and more comfortable for passengers and crew. Her plane disappeared over the Pacific on July 2, 1937, never to be seen again.

The mystery surrounding her death fired people's imaginations, and Earhart became a legend. To this day no one knows how she died.

SPEEDING TOWARD WAR

In the years between the two world wars, the United States, Britain, France, Russia, Italy, and Germany began developing military aircraft.

When Germany, under the direction of Adolf Hitler, occupied the Rhineland in 1936, and Italian aircraft attacked Ethiopia, world leaders had to admit that another world war was at hand. Government orders for military aircraft flooded airplane manufacturers in Europe and the United States.

It was a sign of the times that when the airline of South Africa, South African State Railways, ordered four Envoy commercial planes from Britain's Airspeed Ltd. in the beginning of 1936, they requested that the planes be convertible for military use. Airspeed provided bomb racks and a mounting for a forward firing gun, and the roof of the lavatory could be detached and replaced with another which carried a gun turret.

The Spanish Civil War broke out in July 1936, and Germany used the occasion to test their best fighter and bomber planes. The Messerschmitt Bf109 fighter was one of the planes the German air force, the Luftwaffe, tested in the conflict. The lessons learned in the war resulted in the improved Bf109E version, which proved to be superior to all but the best Allied fighters in the first year of the Second World War.

Another type of plane Germany tested in Spain in 1936 was the Junkers Ju87 Stuka dive-bomber. Three years later, on September 1, 1939 three Ju87s attacked Polish troops around the bridge over the Vistula River in Tczew, Poland. The Stuka's distinctive high-pitched scream marked the beginning of World War II. The German raid also let the world know that whoever ruled the sky would win this war.

THEN AND NOW

After the war, air travel became an accepted part of life for large numbers of people. The gracious, luxurious flying boats stayed around for a few years, but they belonged to an earlier era, when time and money were more expendable.

Travel by air is commonplace now. The rumblings of jet engines are as familiar and as unconscious to the seasoned airline passenger as the sound of their own heart. We forget that once upon a time, the sight of an airplane could make people's hearts skip a beat. But there are still a few aviation old-timers around, and there are always stories to be told about the struggles and wonder of the time when flying was new.